Aspire

Aspire works with people with spinal
cord injuries to create opportunity,
choice and independence.

www.aspire.org.uk

1

Foreword

Aspire prides itself in providing practical help to people who have been paralysed by spinal cord injury. Our Services have developed over many years through working with, and understanding the needs of, those who find themselves in this situation. We aim to be there from the moment someone is injured through to their living an independent and fulfilled life.

Our Independent Living Advisors are all former spinal cord injury patients and have 'been there and done it'. They are professionally trained to give guidance as to how someone newly injured can go on to lead an independent life, whilst also sharing some of their own experiences.

We appreciate that, with such long stays in a Spinal Injury Centre or General Hospital, getting back home is so important. As Jan says in her story, "I just wanted to get home, get the family back together, get on with life." Not every home is accessible, and making the necessary adaptations can cause further delays. We do our very best through the Aspire Housing programme to get people close to home and reunited with their family as soon as possible. In one of our fully accessible, furnished and equipped houses you really can start to 'get on with life'.

The Aspire Assistive Technology programme provides those with limited or no upper limb function with the ability to independently access computers. Over the years we have supported hundreds of people to return to education or employment, stay in control of their financial affairs, keep in touch with family and friends and do their shopping online. Technology plays a huge part in all our lives and such a Service is, as Ryan puts it in his story, 'a lifesaver'.

Whatever you do with your life, having the right specialist equipment can make a big difference. Aspire Grants offers financial contributions towards equipment that would otherwise be out of reach, but without which life would be that much harder or reliant on others.

The stories in this book demonstrate that although things are different after an injury, every day challenges can be, and are, overcome. In that, it becomes a valuable addition to our existing Services.

Aspire is proud to do what we can to help along the way.

Brian Carlin
Chief Executive

When I was asked to feature in the last Aspire Book, *It's My Life*, I did so with some trepidation. It's not easy to talk about yourself, to share stories that might open you up to embarrassment, feelings of intrusion or, worse, charges of self-absorption! So I speak with experience when I say a heartfelt thank you to the 25 people who gave up their time to tell their stories and share their experiences for *It's My Life 2*.

Like me, I suspect many of them will initially wonder just how useful their contribution will be. But reading their stories, I have no doubt that they will have a huge impact on all those who pick up this book. Those featured here are not claiming to be remarkable; their stories instead are about hanging out the washing, returning to work, raising a family and all those every day things that occupy all of our lives. Yet for that, they are remarkable.

These are the things that matter to all of us, and are also those things that when you are first lying in a hospital bed you wonder if you will ever be able to do again.

We hope that whatever reason you have for reading the stories in these pages that they begin to answer your fears and shine a light on the spirit that lives within us all.

David Edwards
Aspire Chairman

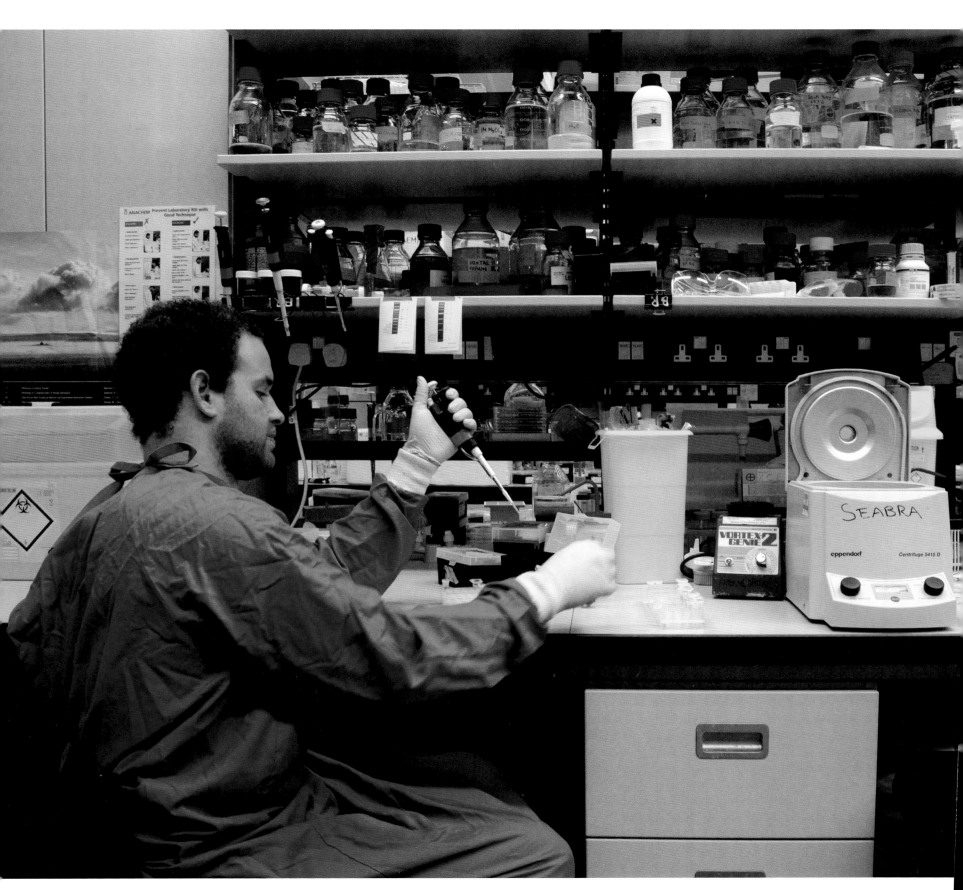

When you have a spinal cord injury and start talking about education, there's this assumption that you'll want to do IT. Fair enough if that's what you are into, but I got that from so many people and I don't even like computers!

I was in the middle of my GCSEs when I was injured. I tried to carry on with the year whilst I was in hospital but with everything else going on it was just too much. I re-sat later, then got a job with the NHS and, whilst there, did my A-levels at night-school. It was a struggle at the time, going to classes nearly every night straight after work, but being a wheelchair user didn't make things any harder. I don't think I had any access issues, there was even a height adjustable lab bench for me to use. And it was worth the effort when I was then accepted by Sussex Uni to do Molecular Medicine.

When I told the University that I was disabled, they invited me down to an interview to talk about any help I might need. Support was always available; things just went very smoothly the whole time I was there. I made adjustments to how I worked, particularly in the lab where I kept my materials on lower shelves. And I put hot samples into a polystyrene box on my lap so that I could still push around the lab safely.

University isn't just about work and I went out quite a lot if I'm honest. Socially, it was great! One of the things that the University did for me was to let me stay in Halls beyond the first year, recognising that it would be hard for me to rent an accessible student house. It made my second year very unproductive – all the new students came in and I basically relived the fresher's experience! At the end of the year I scraped through the exams and realised I needed to up my game. I wouldn't change it, though, it was a great time.

I did pass that third year, and I've since done a Master's at Imperial too. I'm applying for PhDs now, and enjoying having a bit of time to myself. There's loads of support available in education, and you shouldn't be put off just because you have a spinal cord injury. I've heard people say they'll have to change courses now they're injured, but my degree was very practical-based and there was never an issue. With a few changes I'm sure you can do anything, whatever the practical or physical aspects involved, so definitely do what you want and don't let your injury hold you back.

don't let your injury hold you back

It pisses me off every single day that I'm in a wheelchair. I'd give in if it didn't, stop taking on challenges and doing things every day.

I've had the business since '91. I wasn't sure I was going to keep it, but it was all I'd known; I'd done it before the accident, there was nothing to stop me doing it now. I did put someone else in charge for six months and went to Thailand, but I got sick of sitting on a beach and came back to take over.

Before, I would never ask anyone to do anything I wouldn't do myself. That's always been a part of my business, and it still applies now. Modern trucks are automatic anyway, so I can whack hand controls on and drive them. I mostly go out at weekends when the office is quiet, or if a driver can't do a job. I drive all the forklifts in the yard too.

'Nothing I can't do that you can do', is my motto. It might take us longer, I might have to work out a way of doing it, but I'll get it. And you learn all the time. I paid for a hoist for one of the trucks when I first came back. It worked, but it was slow and you'd end up with an audience, everyone standing around watching. Now, the main way I get into the cab is by getting on the forks of a forklift and getting one of the lads to raise me up.

We go all over, getting machinery to Norway, 20 tonne drilling pipes down to Gatwick and onto the planes, helicopters to Luxembourg, even over to the Ukraine. We do more international trips when oil prices are high and the companies are pumping loads and needing new equipment. You can see the recession through our work, but we've still got lots of work on ourselves.

I took a call recently for a last minute job getting a delivery from South Shields up to Aberdeen; none of the other drivers were around, so I did it. The parcel was in the car and I was on my way within an hour.

I've got arms like Popeye now. It's a big thing for me as it means I don't need as much help. I can lift my chair into the car one-handed – even the biggest lad in the yard can't do that.

Being disabled and running my business has been a hindrance. But it's also been a help. I learnt who my friends were when I had my accident; business contacts I'd dealt with for 20 years but had never met were coming to see me. And people remember me, I always get the work. But that's also because I'm good at what I do, and if we're going to do a job we're going to do it properly. People remember bad jobs.

'Nothing I can't do that you can do'

People have said that my positive outlook and stubbornness got me through; my own thinking is that being a little thick and not being able to comprehend the seriousness of the injuries had just as much to do with it! In those first few weeks I was convinced that I would recover totally and be able to look back on that period in hospital with my injuries no longer a problem. I've since had to change my opinion.

My spinal injury is high-level but incomplete and, as such, I have been able to recover the use of my legs. Even so, the injury has still had a huge impact because although my legs have recovered enough to be functional, my upper body, arms and hands are still significantly weaker.

I am an advocate of goal planning. I have always liked to have a target to aim for, and it's something that I've always done, particularly in my professional life. So I related that to what I was facing after my injury. I work with short, medium and long-term goals; regardless of the time frame, if you've set a target you have to be positive if you are going to get there, you can't be flippant. Right from when I was first injured I was seeing progress towards and beyond the goals that I

stubbornness got me through

was setting, and the satisfaction from that helps push you on.

I'd love to run a marathon, but a goal like that would do me more harm than good. So you look at things realistically and you readjust your sights. I do run and I completed a 10km race, although I wouldn't call it running more like a fast shuffle – it was still rewarding and I didn't come last! Most of my goals are about achieving normality, but there are times you have to accept getting as close as you can. You compromise, you change what is normal.

Inevitably, you start to plateau in your progress at some point. It doesn't mean that you give in, though. So I still get frustrated and angry at not being able to complete the simplest of tasks but I've become rather adept at problem solving and finding other ways to do things. I've had to come to terms with the conflicts of everyday life, such as choosing between my work as a police officer and the need to look after myself. It's a balancing act, reducing my work hours, going to the gym every day to keep myself fit and mobile, allowing for the effects of medication. Ultimately, those daily acts and efforts lead to the long term goal of living a good quality life.

I was a police officer when I was injured. It's a job that consumes you; I ate, breathed and lived it, and so much of my identity came from being a police officer. I was injured in the May, and by the following January I was back in work but the wheels were already in motion to discharge me on a medical pension. I know they were trying to look after me, but it was done in a clumsy way and I was really disappointed.

Instead of getting frustrated I looked at what I could do and how I could reinvent myself. I definitely like a challenge and I get bored if I stay doing one thing for too long; over the years I've reinvented myself a few times! I did a sport science diploma and ran my own personal training business, worked for a local authority getting children into sport, trained and worked as an OT both at a Spinal Centre and in the community and then managed a mentoring programme at a charity.

My latest reinvention is as a bike mechanic. I've always been into cycling, before my injury on BMX and mountain bikes and then as a hand-cyclist. I was commuting long distances to work in an office and I was missing out on my young son growing up. I wanted a way I could look to simplify life a little bit. Like all cyclists I had my favourite bike shop and a chance conversation with the owner led to him offering me a job there and then. When I called my wife to tell her, she wanted to know about the hours, salary and so on, all the details I hadn't been bothered about as I was too excited!

Being disabled is totally irrelevant, it's all about the skills you have.

I've always liked getting my hands dirty, and I like the quick gratification that comes from repairing something, from solving a problem and using your own knowledge to put it right. Being disabled is totally irrelevant, it's all about the skills you have. It can be difficult to get a heavy bike up onto the stands and the realities of a busy bike shop is that there is always crap all over the place that can get in the way – but someone will come and give a hand if I holler.

I'm in the right job for me at this time, but who knows when I might fancy another challenge. It's not always easy, I've had my fair share of knock backs and you do have to be resilient. But everything is possible.

I've only been doing it for
about seven months,
but I already hold a couple of
Scottish records.

I was really nervous about going back to school. I didn't know how people would react and I wasn't sure I wanted to go back to the same school where everyone had known me before. But a friend told me that I wasn't allowed to leave, and it was probably the best thing that I did. My friends all stood by me and it was great to be back with them – except when they were telling me to get out my chair so that they could have a go!

The teachers were a bit wary at the start, I think they weren't sure how I was going to react to things. They were overly protective, so they'd be shouting, 'No, no!' across the room if I did a backwheel balance. And it also meant they let me get away with murder. That was quite nice at times, but really I just wanted to be treated like everyone else; I don't get away with much now. I was lucky that it is a new school so there haven't been any issues with getting around the building.

I missed so much school when I was in hospital that it was hard to catch up. I'm doing Highers in Maths, English and Biology – it's my last year at school, and then I'll take a year out and go to Australia or something like that and come back to University. And, of course, I'll continue racing.

Before the accident I did lots of sports, but nothing really competitive. I went to the Spinal Games at Stoke Mandeville and it was really good, getting to try all the different sports. It was wheelchair racing that I really took to, though. I've only been doing it for about seven months, but I already hold a couple of Scottish records. I really enjoy travelling around Britain for the competitions and meeting new people. One of my friends has the biggest crush on David Weir so she was really excited when I met him! Most people are really happy to chat to you, but sometimes they don't take it so well when I beat them and they hear how long I've been doing this for!

And then it's Rio.

I train before and after school, and on Sundays too. I get Saturdays off – unless I'm competing. It's not too hard to fit it all in, the worst thing is going out on the roads when it's still dark. But I'm not an inside person anyway, I don't like being stuck indoors and I've always been up early to help dad on the farm. He comes with me on his bike in the evenings too.

It's the Commonwealths in Glasgow in 2014 and I've got a qualifying time for that already. I'll have to do it again when the qualification process opens, but it'll be exciting to compete in our home Games. And then it's Rio. I'm not going to stop until I get that gold medal.

If you'd have told me 20 years ago that I'd own a caravan, I think I'd have been physically sick. I'd certainly have launched into a diatribe about snails on the motorway. Things change though.

Nineteen years ago I was injured when I fell off some steps in the garden. After seven months in Salisbury, we wanted things to get back to normal for the kids. We'd always gone on camping trips and so we just got the tent back out and had our family holidays again. As the kids grew up and stopped coming away with us, and as the tent gathered more holes, we had a desire for more comfort – you could say it was a product of old age! We've always liked moving around the country and having our weekends away together so we looked at using Bed and Breakfasts. But it was awkward to find out which ones were accessible and so we turned to caravans.

For all my initial fears, a caravan is preferable to a tent; it's easier to pitch, it comes with central heating, and there's a fridge to put the beers in. It took quite a while to find one big enough for the wheelchair, but eventually we got one and adapted it –

the doors were widened, we trimmed down the furniture so I could get sideways on for transfers and set up the ramps. It's got everything I need and there's still plenty of room so I'm not squeezing through gaps or having to reverse. And because it's ours, we can go anywhere in the country and always know we'll be OK to stay there. Basically, it's taken the stress out of getting accommodation, which

I can always get the handbike out for a ride along the tow path

is a huge bonus for my wife as that was always her job.

We've recently found a place to hire accessible canal boats which has given us another brilliant holiday option. Half a dozen of us will go away for the week and the pace of life drops away. You can just sit there and watch the world go by at 3 miles an hour. You see the countryside from a different perspective, and when I'm feeling too sedate I can always get the handbike out for a ride along the tow path. And, brilliantly, you can't be drunk in charge of a boat!

We're expecting our first grandchild next year. Knowng that we'll be able to go away as a family is brilliant. Taking them with us in the caravan or on the boat is going to be great fun.

We've got six children between us, and it was tough on them, me being in hospital so long. They couldn't come and see me that easily, but we did speak on the phone a lot. All told, I was in Stoke Mandeville for 11 months and I just wanted to get home, get the family back together, get on with life.

In that first week back, the children went out of their way to help – I think they were telling each other they mustn't do anything to make mum upset, that they had to keep everything tidy. But it didn't last long! I remember them sitting there watching me struggle with the hoover, trying to plug it in, and instead of jumping up to help they said, "How long are you going to be?" After that, they literally just treated me like nothing had happened. In a way that's my doing; I'm quite a stubborn person, and a glass half full person too. As a family we work through the tough times, we're very capable, and it's stood us in good stead.

It might take me longer, but I do everything that I did before; ironing, gardening, cooking, taking the dogs out, acting as counsellor, doctor, laundry and bank to the children. I've found that you have to plan ahead a bit more, and you have to have a bit of patience. When hoovering, I've had to give up the Dyson and now use a Hettie – like the Henry, but in pink! I push with one hand, hoover with the other, and then swap to get around. My real eureka moment came when I first did the washing again. I think I smiled all the way from taking it out the machine to hanging it up, and then I went in and phoned up a couple of friends to tell them what I'd done! It sounds crazy, but my friends understood – they said it was like having the old Jan back.

As a family we work through the tough times

I soon had all the practical things sorted, but the one thing I found it hard to get my head around was bodily functions not working how they used to. I used to cry when I had to get changed all the time. But once you get your head around it, you see it's part of being paralysed, and it's OK. Like anything, it's about how you deal with it, you have to know it's not your fault.

I used to be a pefectionist, but I'm more accepting and relaxed now. I get nerve pain and spasms, and when I get worked up it really hurts me – so I'm a calmer person as a result! And I've also come to realise that you shouldn't worry about the stuff you can't do, and be thrilled about the things you can.

I'd heard about a charity that works with you to train your own dog to be an assistance dog

My dog can't do the washing up, but that's OK because I have a wife for that. The dog does do a huge amount for me though – he'll pick things up that I drop, take my coat off, fetch things I need, pick up the phone and open and close doors. When you've broken your neck and can't grip anymore, that's a huge help.

He's a Springer Spaniel called Jerry. My wife and daughter got him from a rescue centre; you never know the history of a dog from rescue places, but we do know that he'd been abused. He definitely landed on his feet when he came to live with us and now he's a part of the family.

I'd heard about a charity that works with you to train your own dog to be an assistance dog and it appealed straight away. There was an initial few weeks of training, and then we had to go back for monthly assessments. Jerry was very easy to train as he'd do anything for food!

As a qualified assistance dog, Jerry can be with me pretty much 24/7, even in the cabin of the plane when we go on holiday. The first time we took him on a flight he curled up and went to sleep under my seat, and on takeoff slid along the floor and ended up in the row behind us. I think the people there were a bit surprised as you don't usually see dogs on planes, but he's a little cutie and everyone succumbs to him. We used to fly quite a bit and the cabin crew all got to know him; where we'd be buying our meals, they'd be giving him any that were left over. He'd just roll on to his back and let the stewardesses make a fuss of him.

The one thing I wish is that he was a little bit taller as he's too short to take the money out of the cash machine. I can punch the numbers into the pad, but can't grip the notes so have to ask a passerby to help. He's not like a guide dog, in that I might not have something for him to do every day, but when I need him he's there. One of his tasks is to go and get my asthma inhaler which is kept by the side of my bed. I can be anywhere in the house and he'll go and get it and put it on my lap. When you are gasping for breath you don't mind that there might be a bit of dog slobber on it!

Jerry is there for me when I'm at my most vulnerable, when I'd be stuck without him. But even when he's not working, he's really good for me as we have to get out of the house twice a day for walks. Too many people stay indoors all the time and forget that there's a life out there.

My dog can't do the washing up

I generally don't tell clients that I use assistive technology to work, it's just not necessary. It's about the work I do, not my disability.

When I was in the Spinal Unit, my OT introduced me to the Headmaster system. It tracked your head movements, and you had a mouthstick that you blew into to click. When I left the Unit I attended a local college to do a computer course, and after that I just started buying as many computer magazines and books as I could, doing the tutorials in them and just teaching myself. Now I'm using the SmartNav system, with a couple of big buttons velcroed to my chair that I can just hit with my limited arm movement.

I applied to do design at University but they told me I didn't have enough qualifications. I was a little bugger as a kid and got myself expelled from three schools – the only time I wasn't looking to abscond was when we had an art lesson. Looking back now, not being taught formally was a good thing, I've not been brainwashed into using established techniques and I've been forced to try my own thing. There's so many training videos online that it's often the best way to learn anyway, and now I've done a few tutorials myself to help other people.

Back then I was entering competitions in magazines, and winning quite a few of them, so people started telling me I should be doing this as a living. I got my portfolios together and sent them out. The work is pretty varied – websites, reports, magazines, and I've illustrated a couple of children's books too, one on spies and one on monsters of the deep! The publishers gave me the concept, but I had the creative freedom to come up with the finished graphics. I also do a bit of landscape gardening, but I like to have full control over every aspect of the project and with gardening I'm reliant on others to create the finished garden from my designs.

Working as a freelancer means it's either feast or famine, there's too much work or not enough. I do find myself getting depressed when I haven't got enough work or projects going on. But I like working in my own time as I could never manage a 9-5, and the fact that I can work around any problems that do crop up. Assistive technology has been a lifesaver, it's made all this possible. It took a bit of time to get used to, but with perseverance it's just become second nature.

Assistive technology has been a lifesaver

When I was in court to get custody, the judge said, "Tell me how you can love your children if you can't pick them up." I looked him in the eye and replied, "Love comes from the heart."

I've had 33 years of my spinal injury. In them days, there were no services like there are now. It was just a pat on the shoulder and, 'you'll be alright, Richard' as you left the hospital. My goal was never just to learn to cope, my main priority was my children. No way was Social Services going to take them away.

At first I had a District Nurse come in to help with my daily routine. You had no say in how they worked, you just had to wait and they'd turn up when they could. Often, they'd give you a suppository, go off for a couple of hours, come back and say, 'nothing's happened, I'll come back tomorrow'. So you'd get dressed, have an accident and no one was around to help. There was nothing available in the evenings or through the night – we had a night-sitter but she wasn't allowed to help.

I wanted to be more independent; it was important for the children, to make sure they could have a normal home life. Getting your own PA was a new idea, but if you don't take a risk, you'll never know if it'll work. At first I advertised in the job centre, then used medical students from Denmark who wanted placements as part of their studies. I'm still in touch with some of them, and they're doctors and physios now.

I've learnt that you have to vet very carefully; people say they can do things, but they turn out not to have a clue. And it gets a bit worrying when you are let down; it happened one Christmas, but I sent some texts out and got someone in. Over the years I've had one or two people who've not worked out, but really I've been very lucky.

The most difficult thing has probably been the driving! Most of my PAs come from abroad and it takes some of them a while to remember we drive on the left. And you have to watch their speeding – they think they're still driving in kilometres an hour! I've managed to talk our way out of a few tickets, but not all of them.

Sorting out my own care meant that I could go to meetings at the school, we could go on holiday as a family, we could do all those things that you realise are important when you can't do them. Now I've got seven grandchildren and being independent means they know that Granddads can still go to the park!

my main priority was my children.

It was suggested that we might need to move, but June's father built our house and we've lived in it since we were married 48 years ago. There's a lot of emotional attachment, and adapting it for me now was definitely what we wanted to do.

Right from day one I was told to make sure that I got everything I needed in order to get my lifestyle back. That's alright in essence, but when you first come to look at it you don't know at that stage what it is you want or need. Then, when you start looking at plans you hit the negativity from the planners; 'you can't do this, you can't do that'. You fight that and get on but then, having mapped out exactly what we wanted, you get told you might not be allowed it all because of the expense! It's all coming together now, though.

When I first came out of Salisbury I moved back home where my life existed solely in the lounge and the kitchen. We lived like that for over a year. It was frustrating at times, I definitely felt trapped. But we coped, helped greatly by the support I had from my family, friends and the local bowls club. With the building works due to start, we moved into an Aspire bungalow where I could get all around and do things in the kitchen. Friends were happy too as I could have my first shower in year – they told me I smelt much better afterwards!

We go back to our house once a month for a meeting with the architect and the builders. That's been really helpful as we can always voice any concerns, but actually we've been really quite pleased with it all. The builders have kept to their word and it all seems to be going to plan. We're having quite a lot built on to the back to take a new bedroom, bathroom and a bigger kitchen. All the doorways will have to be widened. And there will be a lift too, so I can get upstairs again. Most of it is reorganising what is already there, so the building is retaining its character, it will still be our home.

Going back home when it's finished, and being able to get into every room in our property, is going to give me a whole new lease of life. The day we go back is going to be emotional for all of us. I've got mixed feelings about it because whilst I'm looking forward to it, I'm doing so with understandable apprehension. That said, I know it will be a great moment.

they told me I smelt much better afterwards!

My first PA lasted less than two weeks. We were assured that she had experience of working with people with spinal cord injury, but when she didn't know what a leg bag was we had our doubts. Later that first week she called my wife at work to ask her what I'd like for lunch. I was sitting in the front room at the time, and my wife suggested the PA might like to ask me! I remember my wife coming home that evening and being upset, it was hard for her going to work knowing that the person who was meant to be looking after me didn't know what she was doing.

It is extremely difficult to have a stranger in your house all the time. And it's harder for my wife and son, getting up in the morning and having a stranger there, coming home after work or school and them still being there. My wife also got quite jealous, knowing that they were with me from the moment I got up to the moment I went to bed, seven days a week.

Our response is to make sure that our PAs are part of the family. We want them to come shopping with us, to eat with us, to be involved in the conversations at the dinner table. It means we're all a part of each other's lives. I know that some people prefer their PAs to disappear at times, to go and hide in their rooms, but that's not the way we like it. They're away from their families too and deserve to be a part of things and have your support. I had two young Australian PAs for a while; they were here to look after me, and my wife wanted to look after them! It created a very strange dynamic, but we all talked about it and found it highly amusing. They're back in Australia now but we still keep in touch with them.

When I first came home I'd already accepted that we'd have to have new people living with us. My wife didn't find it that easy, especially at the weekends when she likes a lie in and I have PAs coming in to help me get up, but she knows it's necessary and so she'll put up with it. At the end of the day, there's not much that either of us can do about the intrusions. Whether you are rich or poor, disabled or not, life is a compromise; this is no different. And the overriding factor is that I'm at home, living a normal life, with my family. The sacrifice is just that someone else has to come into our bedroom every now and then.

> ## It is extremely difficult to have a stranger in your house all the time.

I was in the Parachute Regiment, so was incredibly fit and healthy. I was serving in Afghanistan and the work we were doing meant that you just burnt the fat off. All the weight I had was muscle. I came round in hospital with no movement from the neck down and I wasted away.

The food in hospital was rubbish so I was getting take-aways sent in; Chinese, kebabs, pub food from up the road. I was still skinny when I left, I could still get into all my old clothes, but I'd got into the habit of eating crap food and just carried on; take-aways for dinner rather than going shopping and getting food in, a pasty or pie for lunch. I'd led a really physical life and you don't appreciate straight away how few calories you need when you're not as active, particularly when you use a wheelchair.

I've always taken pride in how I look, I like to look good, and using a wheelchair doesn't change that. But there I was in photos, with my shirt straining across my belly, and the tight collar pushing all the fat on my neck up and over the collar. I looked like a walrus! My OT doesn't hold back; she gave me a kick up the jacksie and told me I needed to do something.

My brother lost lots of weight on a diet he'd found so I joined him on that. You do three days on a low calorie diet and eat healthily the rest of the week, with maybe a bit of a reward of a few beers or a take-away on one day. My injury is incomplete so I also started using the exercise bike. It became a part of my routine, and I stuck to it.

I lost nearly 3 stone, and took 8 inches of my waist. I feel better for it, and I look better for it too; I like what I see in photos now and all my clothes fit. More than that, it's so much easier for me and the carers now when I'm moving or manoeuvring around the bed. At physio, I can bring my legs up without my stomach getting in the way. And where I was filling my wheelchair and pushing against the sides, I'm now comfortable in it again.

I rarely weigh myself, but I keep an eye on my measurements. Because I eat a normal, healthy diet, the weight has stayed off. I'm now an advocate about it all – I don't have time for people who say they cannot do anything about their weight. I look at them and say, 'if I'm in a wheelchair and can do it, what excuse do you have?'

> # I like to look good, and using a wheelchair doesn't change that

We were engaged when I had my accident, and we'd always known that we were going to try for children at some point. Initially, we were concerned that the injury might stop that, but the staff at Stanmore let us know very early on that it wasn't going to affect anything.

When I was pregnant, the GP and midwife asked me if I could have a natural birth; I thought they'd be able to tell me! I was really surprised at how little they knew, I presumed they'd seen people with similar injuries before, and it did make us a bit worried. Stanmore were really helpful, although even there we had differences of opinion, but locally there wasn't much that was reassuring. In the end, of course, it was all OK and Holly was born early which took away the need for a decision about a natural birth or caesarean anyway.

Buying a pushchair was an absolute nightmare. My injury affects my hands and I just couldn't fold most of them down. We went to lots of different shops, and the staff tell you that they have easy to use, single hand mechanisms, but that didn't mean I could do it. It was frustrating to see one we liked, be told it was easy to use, and then not be able to work it. It took

some of the excitement away. We did find one, though, and my other half, Shane, built an adaptation so that it fits on to my wheelchair – I need one of those 'long vehicle' signs when I'm using it, but it means that Holly and I can go out together.

Because of my hands I was worried about how I'd handle Holly, and how I'd manage generally. When we were in hospital I felt really self-conscious with everyone standing around and looking and I left a lot of it to Shane; I wanted to try things without an audience. And yes, things are a bit more difficult, but it's actually all fine, there haven't been any problems. We've put a fridge and bottle warmer upstairs as well as down so at night it's easier and quicker to get to; we've coped really well. She's a great baby; it's tiring, but a good tiring.

I think anyone who is having a baby is nervous, perhaps we were just concerned with different things. As Holly grows I'm going to have to start thinking about whether I'll be able to keep up when she decides to run off...hopefully she'll learn not to! And her getting heavier may present some issues. We've learnt, though, that you can always adapt things and come up with ways that work. It's all going to be interesting and fun.

it's tiring, but a good tiring.

I was lucky to survive the accident and I was in hospital for a long time. When I did begin to tentatively get out of bed, simply wheeling around on smooth hospital floors was hard-going. Just to have independence outside hospital appeared to me to be the ultimate challenge, and so thoughts of having a worthwhile job, a wife and children were almost fanciful. As time went by, my resolve strengthened and aspirations were rekindled. I returned to my studies, qualified and now work as a hospital doctor treating people with cancer.

you presume that you can't father children

What has given me the most joy, though, is getting married and having a beautiful daughter. At first you presume that you can't father children, but we got specialist fertility advice, both from the Spinal Unit and from a fertility clinic locally. The Spinal Unit were key in that they know far more about the specific issues for people with spinal cord injury. Had we just gone to a generic fertility clinic it would have resulted in a more invasive technique and protracted journey. The straightforward and tactful advice from the Unit enabled us to become very happy parents of an adorable baby girl less than two years later.

Spinal cord injury causes impairment and challenges you, but in many other ways you are no different to anyone else. You have the same wants and desires for life, and like any parent you are nervous and excited for your child. Lily doesn't treat me any differently, though if I ask her for a hand she'll proudly push me along. Her friends just think of me as Lily's dad and I think that's good, they're seeing that disabled people can do things. It's the adults that make assumptions about your capabilities; one morning my mother-in-law took Lily to school and one of the other mothers asked where I was. When she was told I was at the clinic that morning, her face took on a look of knowing sympathy; then on being told that actually I was there as the oncologist you could apparently see her recalibrating her whole thought process!

Having an amazing family makes me very happy and my disability doesn't stop me having quality moments with them: enjoying a bit of retail therapy together, wheeling alongside my daughter as she walks to school, sitting next to her as we enjoy a film at the cinema. I treasure these times, so ordinary yet so astounding.

For my first independent holiday after my injury, a friend and I dived head first into the deep end and booked a nine-month round the world trip. We started with backpacking around South-East Asia on a shoestring budget, moved on to Australia, New Zealand, Fiji and Rarotonga, and then did North America in a campervan. Before my injury, I'd only been on a plane a couple of times, but now I've been to something like 48 countries and there are still numerous places I want to visit.

Of course, travelling can be difficult in a lot of ways. When you are away for a long time you need to arrange to have your medical supplies sent out to places along your route. And there will be times when you find yourself needing to be manhandled. But if you take control it'll be OK; sometimes it's what's required to get to those places that you want to see. The less developed countries can be easier than you think – there might be paths full of potholes and accommodation that is far from accessible, but it can be done. A lot of the time, I'll just push down the middle of the road rather than negotiate a bumpy path and local labour is so cheap that you can always hire people to help. In Indonesia a couple of guides got me into the jungle where seeing orangutans in the wild made all the effort worthwhile.

You have to be prepared to leave your comfort zone a bit, and learn what you can and can't get away with. Hygiene is important, but you can bend the rules and reuse catheters and leg bags. You need to get used to being stared at too, and accept that in many cultures it's not considered rude. I volunteered at a Spinal Unit in Bangladesh and so much of the interest stems from their expectation that Western medicine has a cure for everything. Seeing that's not the case, but that you can still have a good life, helped the patients and their families.

Travelling is the most enjoyable experience you can have. We've got a baby on the way so I'm taking a break from it at the moment. In the meantime, just thinking about the high-pitched background street noise in Thailand makes me smile. My friend and I coined a phrase on that first trip: "Damn you, Paradise Island!" It was a reminder that all those little annoying things are probably totally insignificant when you stop and look at your surroundings. Sometimes, you need to quit complaining and get over yourself.

"Damn you, Paradise Island!"

It's hugely frustrating when you're watching porn and the guy comes on and gets into about 20 different positions; you just have to accept that that's not something you can even attempt. It doesn't mean that there's not plenty that you can do though.

I had a girlfriend when I was injured. We stayed together at first, but we were both trying to cope with what we'd lost and I wasn't dealing with things very well. I wasn't the same guy I was before the accident, and I think I just expected her to stick with me regardless; eventually the relationship broke down.

I didn't have huge confidence, and being single didn't help. But I started hanging around with my sister and her friends. I was still coming to terms with the injury, but they were cool with it. The first girl I got together with after that didn't have a clue about spinal injury, and I wasn't sure how to explain just what it all meant, but it was good to be dating again. After that, I had a small succession of girls; it sounds bad now saying that, but it was what I needed. There was nothing serious, they were just short term things, but each was a confidence boost. And I realised that owning up to using a catheter wasn't going to make girls back off.

There have been a few ups and downs relationship wise since then, but I've been with Kelly for a year and a half and things are great. She's never had any issues with some of the grottier sides of my injury and we're confident and comfortable enough together to make things work for us.

I've been asked on a first date before if 'it all works downstairs?' Kelly wasn't so brash, but she's told me since that she'd already run the possible issues through her head. You would, wouldn't you? It's been a concern for me too. But as she says, she's not with me for what I do in bed. Once you are relaxed with someone, the sex is so much better anyway – it's more of a laugh and you're happy to try things. If you are into it, there's all sorts of stuff out there that can help, and peeking into the sex shops in Amsterdam recently was a real eye-opener! I miss the spontaneity; things have to be planned, but the other side is that we're open and talk about what we do and don't want and we've learnt together.

Relationships are hard whoever you are. I might have to throw spinal injury into the mix, but if a girl can't deal with the situation then she's not the right one in the first place.

there's plenty that you can do

It can be harder to meet people when you are out in a really crowded pub or bar. You can sort of find yourself stuck in a corner where the least amount of people will trip over you. But you can always get your friends to start the conversation with the cute guy on the other side of the room and make him come over to you.

My injury didn't stop me meeting new people but I think that, at first, it did leave me a bit reticent about getting to know them. I was still going out, socialising, mixing with people, but I was a bit standbackish. Then, when I started work, it was harder to date anyway – you're always busy, there's all sorts of other stuff going on, and it can be hard enough just to see your friends, let alone spend time with someone totally new.

There's a real body image issue for women now. You want to be attractive, dress well, do your hair and make-up; you want to look your best when you go out. That's no different to what any woman feels. But it's very easy to fall into the trap of thinking, 'they won't find me attractive because I'm in a chair'. You have those thoughts from time to time, and we all need to counter that. We've all got to have self-belief.

I've always been most successful at meeting guys when I'm not actually on the pull anyway, when I'm just being myself. If you look and come across as comfortable and confident then you are much more approachable.

A couple of friends wanted to get me to do speed dating, but that's not my sort of thing. I did contemplate internet dating and I might have gone down that route if I'd not met Paul.

We met on holiday in South Africa. It's a cliché, but he was our tour guide. There was obviously something between us, and I put up with lots of jibing from my friend, but nothing happened during the holiday. When he followed it up after I got home, though, we decided to go for it. Long distance relationships are never easy, but the distance also meant that I had to give him the lowdown on spinal cord injury very early on. If I was going to go and visit, I had to be open about everything. It would have been easy to have avoided that conversation, to put it off as too embarrassing, but Paul made it all very easy. I guess if he was going to have an issue then we wouldn't have lasted anyway.

We're very happily married. It was a big white – and wet! – wedding, with lots of fun, friends and booze.

It's a cliché, but he was our tour guide.

All the way through rehab, Ellen basically lived at the hospital; she learnt about the injury as much as I did. The emotional pain of watching someone you love have an injury is so acute, in many ways I think it's harder than what I was going through. We drew strength from each other and dealt with our pain together.

It never crossed my mind that we wouldn't be together. But we're both ambitious people with lots going on at work so Ellen told me I couldn't propose until she was 26. A month before her birthday I asked her.

A month before her birthday I proposed

I spent a lot of time planning things, I wanted it all to be perfect. And I wanted it to be personal too. I didn't want other people there when I was choosing the ring so I kept leaving my PAs behind when I went to the jewellers. When it came to buying one, the jeweller had to get my wallet out, put the card in the machine and type in the PIN – she was very nervous about being the one to do that!

The wedding was perfect and we had an epic festival-style reception with lots of live music. Ellen and I met at a music festival in Switzerland and we went back to that on honeymoon; there were 14 of us so we didn't get much time alone! We went to San Diego afterwards for a more intimate time.

We've had to remember to develop our own lives so that the situation doesn't end up stifling us. We've got space to do our own things, and it means that I'm not reliant on Ellen; she doesn't have to think of me before she does every little thing. It also means I've had to learn to deal with my own frustrations without burdening her every time, but also keep her involved all the way. It's a delicate balancing act, I need support from elsewhere too – family and friends for emotional support, and PAs for almost everything else. I use live-in PAs, and managing the loss of privacy continues to be a big learning process. We have to make our own space, to engineer time together, and we really value our evenings alone. Communication, as the cliché goes, is the key. We have to be open and honest – with each other, and with the girls who live with us too.

My injury has helped us understand each other. When you go through such an experience, you learn so much and you see how you each cope and what you both need. The emotional bond between us was always strong, now it's even stronger.

A lot of people think that bowls is just an old person's sport. I used to think the same. But once they come along, see the facilities and give it a go, they find that it can get really competitive and addictive. It helps that we get absolution from wearing the whites!

There always used to be a bowls club for disabled people, but the guy who ran it died and the whole thing ground to a halt. I always knew in the back of my mind that there was this fantastic facility just sitting idle right next to Musgrave. When I went over to check it out I saw all these bowling wheelchairs lined up looking very lonely and decided I had to do something about it. I put on a session for a few of the new guys, you know, just trying the idea out to see what would happen. And it was so successful it's just snowballed.

For someone newly injured, it's a great first sport to try – it's nice and easy, there's no danger of picking up any bumps or knocks. But you are still getting out of the hospital, practising your transfers, getting your balance, picking up new skills. The staff from the hospital come along too, it's become part of rehab, and they think it's great. We have about 14 people coming along every month, with a mix of patients and guys who've been injured maybe 10 or 20 years. Once the games are finished, we stick around for an hour or two for some food and a chat. There are a couple of bars there so sometimes you find yourself staying that little bit longer! But the social scene is really the icing on the cake, seeing people mixing, sharing stories and so on, it really adds something.

It was so successful it's just snowballed.

It is a lot of work, organising everything, sorting out the venue, calling people to remind them, working with Musgrave. And now we've got a regular tournament against a club in Dublin, with aspirations for UK wide tournaments too, all of which means more for me to do. But I get to see the difference it makes. I see firsthand how some of the guys in hospital have their heads down, with little enthusiasm for doing anything. And bowls, although it's small, gets them out and trying something new. I'm not fussed about people joining the club long term, but I am fussed about seeing them come along to give it a go. If that gives them the spark to go and do other things that have nothing to do with bowls then that's great, it makes all the effort worthwhile.

A lot of people think
that bowls is just an
old person's sport.

I've always been a
bit of an
adrenaline junkie

I had the tattoo on my stomach done almost as soon as I left hospital. It says, 'Best before 28/09/2003', a reference to the day I had my motorbike accident.

I was living in Tenerife when I had my accident and was loving life. I've always been an adrenaline junkie and there I was riding motorbikes, getting up into the hills to mountain bike and hike, and had a job filming people doing bungee jumps; I'd start each day with a coffee, a donut and a bungee jump.

Everything came to an abrupt end the day I crashed. I sat in hospital depressed that it was all over. I wasn't bothered about being in a chair, I could deal with that, but I just felt I couldn't bloody well do anything to get the adrenaline going. Later I tried all sorts of activities – canoeing, abseiling, getting up into places I'd have presumed inaccessible – and I had a good time. But there was nothing that thrilled me. I did take to wheelchair skills, though, and used to get some protective skateboard gear on and go and take on the steps and ramps in the local park. I'd be backwheel balancing down steps one at a time, knowing that if I got it wrong I'd end up on flat on my face. It gave me a buzz, and got other people thinking I was nuts.

Things changed when I found an outdoor pursuits place in Colorado that did downhill mountain biking. I went over, ignored all the other activities and just biked the whole time, upping the ante each day with longer and faster tracks. I was completely sold. Being out on rough trails again, blasting along, remembering the old mentality of caution being the enemy; it's what I'd been missing. It's a combination of mountain biking and rallying; you need to leave your brain at the top of the hill and use your commitment and skill to get you to the bottom. Of course, you'll find yourself upside down or in a tree at some point, but that just makes me more determined to go again.

I'd once thought I'd never have been able to do again.

Me and another guy started the club, Rough Riderz, to get other people into the sport. We take people out on taster days and every single person has come back absolutely pumped and buzzing. It takes me back, reminds me of the enthusiasm I had that first week when I felt the adrenaline again. We're working on a British made bike to make it more affordable too.

I've just got back from Tenerife where I was back up in the hills with my mates, riding our old tracks and doing something I'd once thought I'd never have been able to do again.

BRIAN

People with my level of injury don't normally get to go home – Lyn broke every rule in the book to get me back. I'm sure they kept my hospital bed warm for me but here we are, living a normal life and doing so very successfully.

At first, nothing was set up to help us. We even had to buy medical equipment on eBay. We've continued to hit the odd snag. When we tried to get physiotherapy sessions in the local hospital, they told us that they didn't have expertise in ventilators and so, for Health and Safety reasons, we couldn't come in. When they phoned to tell us that, we were sitting in a café at the supermarket where I'm pretty sure they also don't have that expertise!

Yes, it's awful what's happened to me. But I don't need now to live in a care home. I've got various bits of technology so I can control my surroundings, we head up to the pub, go and do the shopping, I've got my family around me and right now I'm sitting here looking out over my own back garden. We've had to fight for that every step of the way, but it was worth fighting for and we would do it all again without hesitation.

LYN

Hospitals are so risk averse. But we've always said you have to put risk into perspective – Brian's been to three wars, so living at home isn't what we'd define as a risk.

My background is in solving problems and not accepting what I'm first told. There was a general consensus that Brian would have to go to a nursing home, but we made it clear from the start that his coming home was the only option we would accept. It took us six months of fighting to get it.

The people you are dealing with aren't horrible, but they do like to follow policy. I tried to get as many meetings as possible at Brian's bedside so that they could see him as a person, not just as a name on a bit of paper. If you can build a relationship with them then they want to help, you just have to ease them past their worries and budget constraints.

We've had to break down barriers and get new ways of working in place. The PCT were worried it wouldn't work, but I think now it has they are chuffed. And because we've been trend setting, this will become more common and we'll see many more people on ventilators living at home.

I don't need now to live in a care home

Of course, my lifestyle has changed. But that's because I'm older now, not because of the chair, and that would have happened anyway. Friends have settled down to have kids, and the clubs just don't have the same appeal they had when I was a party girl in my 20s. We all still go out, though, and I still like a drink, it's just that now we have the wine with food! Not everywhere is accessible, but many restaurants, bars and theatres are and on the whole it's pretty good.

Before my injury I hadn't driven for years. I've got no sense of direction and I get very nervous; just reverse parking brings me out in a sweat! But I've got no fear when it comes to public transport. I guess I'm lucky that I live in London where things are a bit more accessible, though things are far from perfect and problems do happen – a simple journey to a friend's birthday party the other day ended up taking me five hours.

But when it works, it's great. I've learnt that you need to be organised and properly plan your journey. When it comes to using trains, you're meant to give 24 hours notice so that they can make sure someone is around with the ramps. But life isn't like that, is it? I hate being tied to a fixed schedule and I resent someone controlling how I should live my life. And when a friend asks if I want to go for a drink after work, I want to be able to go along without worrying how I'll get home again. So I've learnt when you can break those rules; if you know your way, you know there will be people around, then it's probably OK just to turn up. But you have to be sensible, and if you are travelling to a station you don't know or it's late at night, then there's a danger you'll end up not being able to get off the train at your stop.

So much of the underground still isn't accessible. But I'll use the escalators in my chair, as long as I can get two people to stand either side of me. Some platform staff try to stop you, thinking there's a health and safety risk, but I just wait until they're not looking. I'm independent and want to do things for myself so I've had to learn that it's OK to ask for help. I've realised that as long as I'm assertive and that help is given on my terms, I'm still the one in control. After all, asking for help when I need it isn't going to kill me. Of course, I select my potential helpers carefully – if you're going to talk to people on the tube, they might as well be good looking!

I've had to learn that it's OK to ask for help.

I've always loved to travel, so one of my biggest worries when I had my accident was that this would no longer be possible. Fortunately, it definitely is.

When flying, I always book assistance beforehand so they know I'm coming. Plus I make it very clear at the check-in desk that I need an aisle chair to get on the plane. Unfortunately, it still means you often have to have conversations where it takes them a while to really understand what's going on: "So, you can't walk at all?...But you can walk up the stairs if we get you to the bottom of them?...But if we get you onto the plane you can walk to your seat?" It's important to be very clear on what assistance you need.

I also stress the importance of how much I need my wheelchair to be there at the other end. Sometimes on long-haul flights, if you ask nicely, they store the chair in the cabin which is great for peace of mind. Otherwise, just ensure your chair is tagged before it goes into the cargo hold, and it's worth keeping your cushion with you so it doesn't get lost. There have been times when my wheelchair has been sent to baggage reclaim instead of being brought to the cabin on arrival – really not very useful! When it does happen, you have no choice but to go in one of the airport wheelchairs which are huge – I could fit in one three times over!

Even when you do everything right there can still be problems. Once, when flying to Egypt, there was no aisle chair to get me off the plane. They said we'd have to wait an hour. So we took the wheels off my wheelchair so it would fit up the aisle, then my friend held the back up and pushed me towards the obviously astounded - but also impressed - flight attendants!

If you are flying, always ask for a free upgrade. You might not get it but it's worth a try – I make a bee-line for the check-in desk with the most smiley member of staff! And don't forget that with most airlines you can take 'medical equipment' as part of your baggage allowance. Carry important medication in your hand luggage though just in case.

Being on the British Disabled Ski Team, I travel the world. Airline staff look like they are about to have a heart attack when we all turn up – seven wheelchair athletes each with a large bag, a huge long bag full of race skis and an enormous sit-ski. That is the definition of not travelling light! Travelling is sometimes a bit of a hassle, but it's always worth it.

Travelling? It definitely is possible.

There's not always much of an incentive to work again after you've been injured. You don't really hear about how to plan a career when you are in the hospital, it can be left to you to deal with once you're back at home. And you know that a lot of people don't go back to work at all. I think I fell into a bit of a rut of not doing anything and started to get depressed.

I had a lot of friends who were starting new jobs and moving on with their lives and I was embarrassed that I wasn't doing the same. I actually felt a bit pathetic. I knew that I didn't want to just sit at home, I'm not like that and I didn't want society to be paying for me.

Sports and fitness had always been a huge part of my life so I started going back to the gym, being a bit more like my old self. Then I looked for work; there's this perception that if you are disabled, especially if you are in a wheelchair, that you'll have to work in an office. I've always envisaged working in something sporty and I'd be pretty upset if I thought that wasn't now going to happen. Fortunately, I came across Aspire's InstructAbility programme and it was just what I'd been hoping for.

The content of the course was a bit basic for me, but it got me that bit of paper that said I was qualified as a gym instructor. And it was good just to meet the other people on the course, to know I wasn't a one off in wanting this sort of thing. The work placement I did at a local gym was great. It wasn't just about working again, it was also about breaking down barriers. People seem to think that if you are in a chair and not a Paralympic athlete then you must be a bit weak. Yet here I was, showing that disabled people can be in good shape.

There's always going to be some reluctance about using a disabled fitness instructor, people are just unsure whether you can be any good. But that improved, and the more people heard me speak then the more they could tell that I knew what I was talking about. Of course it can be difficult to show people movements, but you can get someone to help with that. So much of being an instructor is about your knowledge and your ability to pass that on and that's not affected by being in a wheelchair.

Gyms can be intimidating places. But the more disabled people work in them, then the more disabled people will use them, and the less intimidating they'll be. Opening those doors has to be a good thing.

I didn't want to just sit at home

Mark Daniels Pages 4/5

Injured at 17

RTA: bus accident

Stanmore: 6 months

T10 incomplete

Brian Wragg Pages 6/7

Injured at 39

Industrial Injury

Middlesbrough: 3 months

T12 /L1 incomplete

Andrew Jackson-Shaw Pages 8/9

Injured at 42

RTA: car accident

Stoke Mandeville: 3 months

C4 incomplete

Steve Hodges Pages 10/11

Injured at 27

RTA : motorbike accident

Salisbury: 5 months

T6

Samantha Kinghorn Pages 14/15

Injured at 14

Accident

Glasgow: 6 months

T10 complete

Badg Champion Pages 16/17

Injured at 40

Fell off steps in garden

Salisbury: 7 months

C7/6 incomplete

Jan Order Pages 18/19

Injured at 48

RTA : motorbike accident

Stoke Mandeville: 11 months

T7/8 complete

Stephen Greenhalgh Pages 22/23 ★

Injured at 27

Diving accident in Greece

Southport: 12 months

C5/6 incomplete

Ryan Forshaw Pages 24/25 ○

Injured at 17

Fell from goal post

Southport: 6 months

C4/5 complete

Richard Spencer Pages 26/27

Injured at 27

RTA: car accident

Stoke Mandeville: 7 months

C5/6 complete

Colin Hudson Pages 28/29

Injured at 71

RTA: car accident

Salisbury: 6 months

C6/7 incomplete

Tim Scott Pages 30/31

Injured at 45

RTA: motorbike accident

Stoke Mandeville: 7 months

C6/7 complete

David Caldwell Pages 32/33

Injured at 31 Gun shot in Afghanistan

Selly Oak: 5 months and

Stanmore: 6 months

C4/5 incomplete

Gabriel Mallon Pages 36/37

Injured at 28

RTA: car accident

Belfast: 3 months

T3 complete

Becky Mason Pages 38/39

Injured at 17

RTA: car accident

Salisbury: 13 months

C5/6 complete

Tom Nabarro Pages 40/41

Injured at 22

Snowboarding accident

Stoke Mandeville: 15 months

C4 complete

James Drennan Pages 42/43

Injured at 23

Motorcross accident

Salisbury: 13 months

C5/C6 complete

Rob Smith Pages 44/45

Injured at 20

Fell from cliff

Salisbury: 9 months

C5/6 incomplete

Natalie Burr Pages 46/47

Injured at 24

Sporting Injury

Stanmore: 4 months

C6 incomplete

Thomas Wells Pages 48/49

Injured at 21

Tobogganing Accident

Salisbury: 14 months

T5/6 complete

Phil Hall Pages 52/53 #

Injured at 31

RTA : motorbike accident

Southport: 3 months

T12 complete

Brian Voce Pages 54/55

Diagnosed at 41

Non-traumatic

Sheffield: 5 months

C2/5 vented

Yasmin Sheikh Pages 56/57

Injured at 29

Non-traumatic

Stanmore: 3 months

T5 incomplete

Jane Sowerby Pages 58/59

Injured at 28

Fall

Stoke Mandeville: 3 months

T10 complete

Charlie Humpreys Pages 60/61

Injured at 21

Skiing accident

Oswestry: 5 months

T10 Complete

Thank you

Aspire would like to thank everyone who has contributed, in whatever way, to making *It's My Life 2* possible.

Photography

All photographhy Max Forsythe

www.maxforsythe.com

+44 (0)20 8948 6888

max@maxforsythe.com

Except photography for

pages 52/53 Louise Bush

www.oohlalapin.co.uk

page 55 Fin Davies

www.imagesbyfin.com

Interviews and words

Alex Rankin (Aspire)

Producer Christine Robinson (Aspire)

Design & Production

Frank Sully & Partners

+44 (0)20 7267 9747

frank-sully@btconnect.com

★ Stephen's dog Jerry was trained by the Sheffield-based charity Support Dogs. Find out more about their vital work at www.support-dogs.org.uk

\# For more information about Rough Riderz, or to book a taster experience, go to www.roughriderz.com.

❍ Ryuneo Designs is a graphic design company that specialises in providing distinctive and cost effective design solutions. http://www.ryuneo.com

An Aspire publication

ISBN 978-0-9563371-1-5 *It's my life 2*

Printing Oriental Press

All proceeds from this book will go to Aspire.

Registered Charity No. 1075317

Scottish Registered Charity No. SC037482

www.aspire.org.uk

Aspire is grateful to Hollister for their kind sponsorship of *It's My Life 2*.

Hollister Continence Care is committed to individuals and to helping them take control of their lives. It begins with understanding a user's needs and applying our tradition of technical advancements and product development. Our products and services are testimony to the assurance that quality of life needn't be compromised by managing one's continence.

Everything we do is informed by the guiding principle: People First.

Hollister are proud to support Aspire.